create your own
free-form quilts

A STRESS-FREE JOURNEY TO ORIGINAL DESIGN

RAYNA GILLMAN

C&T PUBLISHING

Text and Photography copyright © 2011 by Rayna Gillman

Photography and Artwork copyright © 2011 by C&T Publishing, Inc.

Publisher: Amy Marson

Creative Director: Gailen Runge

Acquisitions Editor: Susanne Woods

Editor: Lynn Koolish

Technical Editor: Teresa Stroin

Cover/Book Designer: April Mostek

Production Coordinator: Zinnia Heinzmann

Production Editor: Alice Mace Nakanishi

Photography by Christina Carty-Francis and Diane Pedersen of
C&T Publishing, Inc., unless otherwise noted

Published by C&T Publishing, Inc., P.O. Box 1456, Lafayette, CA 94549

Library of Congress Cataloging-in-Publication Data

Gillman, Rayna, 1941-

Create your own free-form quilts : a stress-free journey to original
design / Rayna Gillman.

  p. cm.

ISBN 978-1-60705-250-0 (soft cover)

1. Quilting. I. Title.

TT835.G57 2011

746.46--dc22

2011015716

Printed in China

10 9 8 7 6 5 4 3 2 1

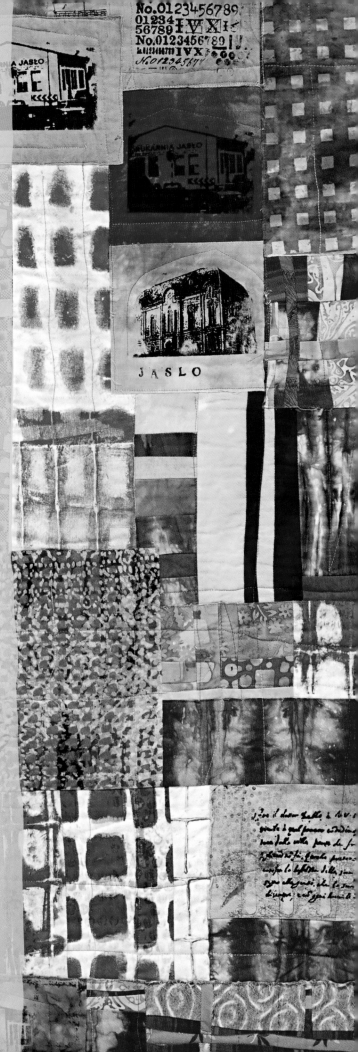

dedication

With love and thanks to Helene, whose long-ago advice to sew therapy strips was the impetus for this book. Over the years, she has taught me more about good design by osmosis than any formal training could have done.

acknowledgments

With special gratitude to Rachel, who agreed to be a guinea pig for some of my UFO (unfinished object) experiments and kept me company when I needed it. To my artist friends, who kept me sane while I juggled book and exhibit deadlines and tried to find time to make art. You know who you are. To Jessica, proofreader extraordinaire, without whom my book would have been much wonkier. And to Marty, who never complained when I left him alone so I could write—all my love, as always.

Special thanks to my intrepid editor, Lynn Koolish, and to the terrific staff at C&T.

You are the best!

contents

introduction

"When all else fails, sew strips," said my friend Helene when I had a bad case of blank design wall syndrome in 2001. She called it therapy sewing, and indeed, she was right. That day, I cut dozens of fabric strips from my stash of hand-dyed and commercial fabrics. Then I sewed my heart out, putting one next to the other without thinking about color or value or what went with what. The "sew don't think" process made me feel immensely better—until the next day, when I was faced with a stack of strips all going in the same direction and looking rather clunky.

Sew-don't-think strips

Out came the rotary cutter again. On impulse, I sliced, diced, added fabrics, and resewed the pieces every which way, repeating the process until the results made me smile.

Slice, dice, and add fabrics.

Three of the pieces became a cheerful nine-patch. I put the rest into a box of blocks and strips left over from previous projects and forgot about them.

Forever Plaid by Rayna Gillman, 18″ × 18″, 2001

Two years later, I came across the box and realized that the unused strip units were perfect additions to the piece I was making.

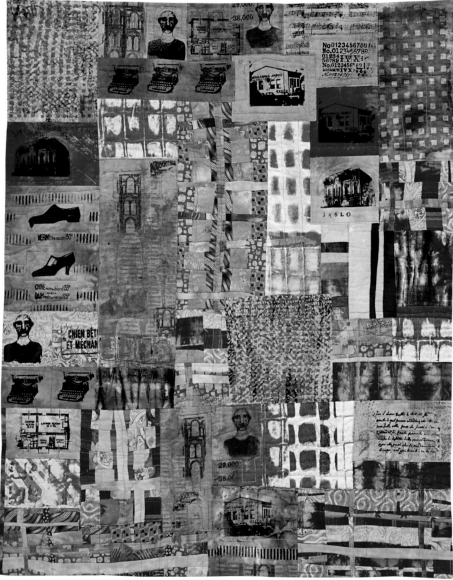

Dwellings by Rayna Gillman, 33½″ × 41″, 2003

The leftovers from *that* quilt went into the box, and every so often, I added more and put it away again. Over the years, every time my muse took a vacation, I sewed strips and threw them into the box without any idea of how I would use them. When I hit a creative low, I took them out, cut them up, remade them, and put them on the wall, designing as I went along. And almost every time, something magical happened.

Recently, faced with a pile of fabrics I couldn't decide how to use or didn't like, I challenged myself to stop printing for a while and *sew*, using only what I had on hand. I cut strips of my hand-prints and combined them with hand-dyes and commercial fabrics. In no time flat, I had made three quilts that I loved. Wouldn't you like to do the same?

In the chapters that follow, you'll see how to make one-of-a-kind units from strips and squares or rectangles, put them together in unexpected combinations, and design new work on the wall. Working "ad hoc" (don't think; just cut, sew, and throw the results into a box until later), you'll discover a new way of using what's on hand to create exciting, original quilts.

how to use this book

This is not a book about how to design an art quilt. There are lots of books that take you through design principles and ask you to apply them using specific exercises and projects. This is a book about making *original* quilts.

I say "original" rather than "art" quilts because I believe the word *original* better defines work you design and create yourself. It doesn't always have to be "art"—though often, it will be.

Perhaps you've dyed, discharged, screened, and monoprinted yards of cloth in a class or in your studio. Or maybe you have been seduced by hand-dyes and hand-prints at a quilt show or on the Internet. The creative (or shopping) process has been fun, but the pile is growing, and you really need to use some of that fabric. In addition, you undoubtedly have a huge stash of commercial fabrics. Can you use all of them together? Of course!

Hand-printed text, Indian batik, and solids

In this book, you'll discover how to use your hand-prints, hand-dyes, commercial stash fabrics, and leftovers to make exciting new work—without patterns, without templates, and without worrying about straight edges, matching seams, or other technicalities.

Even if some of those fabrics are ugly, muddy, or blotchy, take heart! You'll see how to make the most of them.

Use commercial prints, hand-dyes, and hand-prints together.

Use this book as a resource to spark your imagination and to create exciting work without overthinking. The many examples and photos in this book will help jump-start you in a new direction, with the "how to" evolving as you work and evolving differently for you than for anybody else.

You're going to be sewing bits and pieces together into units and larger elements, most of which will be based on strips or squares with simple but quirky variations.

Square-based center panel with strips on each side

Edges will be wonky; seams won't be straight. You can add or delete as you go and not worry about making a mistake. Best of all, the no-rules, no-ruler (almost) way of working is unpredictable and fun.

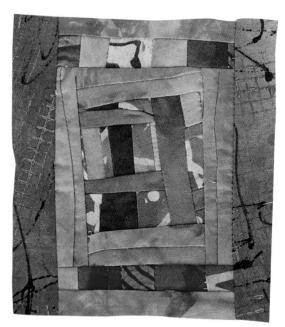

Hand-dyes and hand-prints improvisationally pieced

No-ruler strips have a lot of possibilities.

Blah fabric becomes interesting in funky, improvisationally pieced rectangles.

I hope this book will inspire you to:

- Work intuitively without planning ahead or worrying about where you are going.

- Trust your eye and your instincts to guide you with color and placement.

- Not worry about lines that aren't straight or seams that don't match.

- Delete the word *mistake* from your creative vocabulary.

- Cut without a ruler and use it only for trimming.

- Feel free to combine fusing, raw edge, and piecing in one quilt—in other words, use whatever works in a particular spot.

- Create directly on your design wall.

- Combine hand-printed cloth with other fabrics to create original quilts that are yours, and yours alone.

As with my previous book, *Create Your Own Hand-Printed Cloth,* this is a process book that will take you on a journey where you can play, experiment, and make some detours on the way. The destination will be a surprise, but you'll know when you have arrived.

getting started

Like any pack rat, you probably have a stash of yardage, large pieces, and bags of small leftovers—strips that didn't make it into a Log Cabin, odd-sized scraps left from a baby quilt, blocks that didn't fit, random trimmings from squaring up your work, or last bits of fabric you loved and couldn't bear to part with. In addition, you probably have some unfinished tops stashed away that you think you'll finish *someday*.

get organized

If your sewing room looks like mine, with everything in a jumble, you might want to get organized before you get out the rotary cutter and rev up the sewing machine. Even if your workspace is neat, it might help to do a few things ahead of time.

THROW THE BITS INTO A TREASURE BOX

First, grab a large plastic box and toss in those small scraps and leftover strips. Leave room to add as you go along. Keep a couple of spare plastic storage boxes for the new units you will be creating with those scraps (and your other fabrics).

Small scraps and leftover strips

MAKE A PILE OF LEFTOVER BLOCKS AND UNFINISHED TOPS

Put aside a pile of leftover blocks and unfinished tops, because later you'll work some miracles with them by reinventing them into new, contemporary work.

Leftover blocks and unfinished tops

SORT YOUR FABRICS

Yes, sorting fabrics is time-consuming, but you don't have to do it right this minute. After you've finished reading is time enough. For now, let's see how to make the sorting process easier when you get around to it.

CUT INTO THEM

Yes, cut! As you are sorting, cut into each piece that is larger than a half yard. This is the moment of truth, because we tend to think some of our fabrics are so precious that they are too beautiful to use.

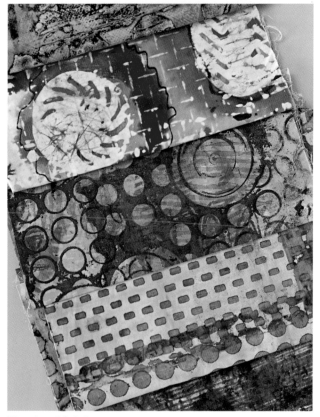

"Precious" fabrics

We believe this of fabrics we've bought and especially of our own hand-printed cloth. We think, "It is one-of-a-kind. I will never make anything so wonderful again." Or, "I only printed a quarter yard. If I had known how it would turn out, I would have made a whole yard." When we do print or buy more fabric, it usually ends up being another interesting or beautiful piece of cloth we can't live without. But is there any point in saving fabrics for the great garage sale in the sky?

I promise, you can get over it. Cut a 6″ strip from every half yard or more you've purchased, dyed, or printed. Put aside those strips and consider the rest fair game to be used. That way you'll have a minicollection of your precious fabric if you ever need to fondle it or, perish the thought, use it again.

sorting commercial fabrics

You might already have your fabrics in neatly sorted piles by type: florals, batiks, abstracts, ethnics, solids, stripes, and so on. Perhaps you have grouped them by color, ranging from light to dark in each category. Or maybe you've put all the fabrics that "go together" (whatever that means to you) in one pile. Fabric manufacturers make this sorting process easy for us because they print fabrics that are coordinated by pattern or color. Even so, it doesn't hurt to shuffle them a bit, because it will help you see your stash with new eyes.

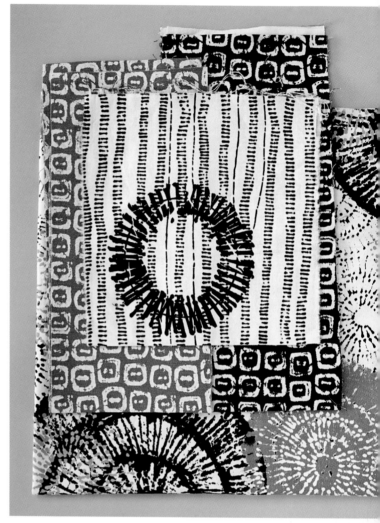

Manufacturer's coordinated collections

sorting hand-prints

Hand-prints are a horse of a different color (if you'll excuse the expression). Because hand-printed fabric is one-of-a-kind and not necessarily designed to go with six other fabrics from the same set, it's a little more challenging to sort. If you don't have any hand-printed or hand-dyed fabrics in your stash, you can still use these methods of sorting for your commercial fabrics. Here are some suggestions that work for me.

sort by color

This sorting will be subjective—sorting printed fabrics that include a variety of colors is often a judgment call. Don't overthink; sort quickly and by intuition. Don't worry, you can always reevaluate when you're done.

Sorting by color—some hand-prints grouped as blue-green

sort by value

Sorting by value without regard to color is an underrated and underused way to categorize. Taking a black-and-white picture with your digital camera can be a great help, because it is much easier to see value when color is not a distraction.

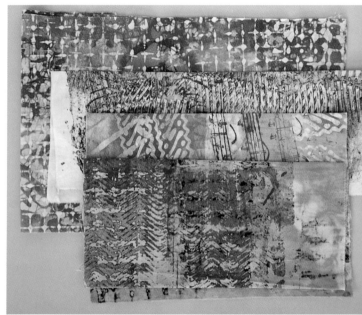

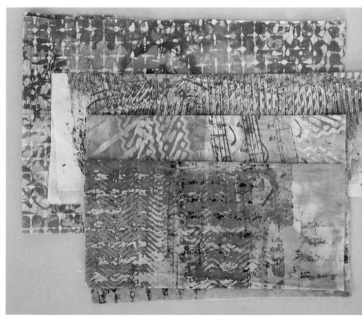

Sorting by value—Black-and-white photo shows these are all medium values.

sort by mood or motif

Sorting by mood or motif makes it easy to see what you have in a category and may give you an idea for a piece or a theme.

Sorting by mood—These fabrics have similar textural feeling and would make good backgrounds or resting places for viewer's eye.

Sorting by motif—All have a strong graphic look, so they might be good cut into small pieces.

mixing it up

You may not feel the need to separate your fabrics by whether they are hand-dyed, hand-printed, or commercial solids and prints. That's fine. Even if you don't want to make the distinction, you can still sort by color, value, and mood or motif.

Sorting by color—combining hand-printed, hand-dyed, and commercial solids and prints

Nothing is set in stone, and you'll probably sort and recategorize your fabrics many times. I often sort by color. Then, when I need inspiration, I iron the fabrics and sort again as I go, perhaps by value or mood. It's amazing how doing this can help me see what I have and envision new combinations. I highly recommend the re-sorting process!

WHAT TO DO
WITH THE UGLIES

While you're sorting your fabrics, make a pile of dogs. These are the pieces you are not happy with: blotchy dye jobs or bad color, fabric you've overprinted so much it is mud, or anything you're tempted to throw away. But *stop!* Don't throw them away. Just put them aside, because there are many ways to use them.

Overprinted ugly fabric

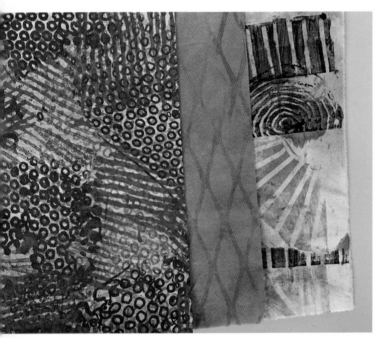
Uglies

cut them into bits and strips

Almost anything looks better in small pieces. Cut strips from those dogs and throw them into your box of scraps.

Strips

use the largest ones for backs

It won't matter what pieces for the back look like; just set them aside. I am always amazed when I use fabric I don't like for the back and somebody tells me it should have been a two-sided piece.

add or remove a layer

Sometimes an additional layer will make all the difference between *blah* and *wow!* Overdye, overprint, or discharge—you can find lots of ways to do this in my book *Create Your Own Hand-Printed Cloth.*

give them away to people who will use them

There's always someone else who will love the fabric you'd like to ditch. Tastes differ, visions of what to do with a piece of cloth differ, and another artist's results with your fabric may make you think twice about having given it away—so save a piece for yourself.

case study of an ugly fabric

Occasionally, a piece of hand-printed cloth will become a wholecloth piece.

But in most cases, you will be combining hand-prints with other hand-prints, solids, hand-dyes, or commercial prints from your stash.

Take this piece of hand-dyed and hand-printed fabric, for instance. I am not a fan of pink, so I gifted pieces of it to several of my students and asked them to use it any way they liked.

Five out of six of my students combined the hand-printed cloth with commercial fabrics from their stash. Here are a few of the ways they used my rejected pink fabric.

"Ugly" fabric

as focus fabric

Two people made it the star of the piece.

Pink-Challenged by Jeanette Davis, 14″ × 14″, 2009

Pinks on Parade by Beverly Hart, 12″ × 13¾″, 2009

as background

Two gave it a supporting role.

in strips

Two made it a bit player.

No Birds … Just Plaid by Carole O'Brien,
12″ × 17″, 2009

Labyrinth by Lynn D. Mattingly, 17″ × 17″, 2010

Rayna's Challenge by Terry Lee, 12¾″ × 9¼″, 2009

Syncopated Jazz by Sandra Hoefner, 23″ × 29″, 2010

Seeing how well these artists had used fabric that I disliked gave me pause, as well as a bit of regret that I'd given most of it away. Luckily, I found another piece and challenged myself to use it. After I had combined the pink with some "therapy strips" and other hand-prints, I couldn't remember why I hadn't liked it.

As you go through this book, you'll use hand-prints, hand-dyes, and commercial fabrics together. You'll discover how to use not only the fabrics you love but also the ones you don't like. The possibilities are limited only by your sense of adventure and your willingness to experiment. Get started now by cutting strips and doing some therapy sewing.

Landing Strip by Rayna Gillman, 15″ × 16″, 2010

start stripping

This is where it all starts. The great thing about sewing strips is that no seams have to be lined up, no corners have to match, and you are free to do what you like.

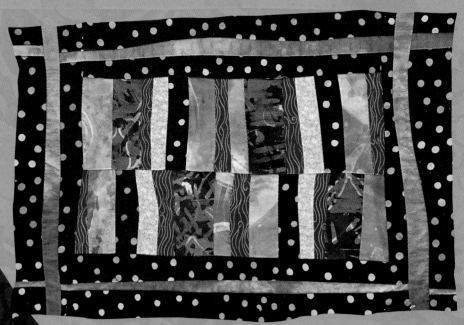

Don't worry about matching seams.

Once you've started, you'll want to keep going. Sewing strips is meditative work; don't worry about what you will do with all of the strips. They will take care of themselves as you go through the book.

gather your tools

- Cutting mat
- Rotary cutter
- Scissors
- Pins
- Thread and sewing machine
- Design wall
- Several empty plastic storage boxes
- Ruler (for occasional use)

put away the ruler

Cutting strips of fabric without a ruler and sewing them together improvisationally is neither new nor original. What *is* new and original is how you can use your own fabric, what you do with the strips after they're sewn into units, and how you combine them to create new elements. It's an exciting way to design an original quilt—no matter what you do, no two will ever be alike.

Usha's Quilt by Rayna Gillman, 39″ × 43″, 2004

cutting strips

Everyone who cuts strips without a ruler and sews them together so they are slightly wonky has his or her own method. If you already work this way, there's no need to change what works for you. If you haven't tried it, I'll explain how I do it. If you find a method that you like better, go for it. In the end, it doesn't matter how you arrive at your destination.

STRIP SIZE

In my book, there is no "should." The length of each strip will vary depending on what is in your scrap box or how long you want it to be.

Presumably, you already have some left-over strips in your plastic treasure box, so that's a good start. Now it's time to add to your inventory.

You can begin by precutting a dozen or so strips of various colors and values using solids and prints—whatever you have close at hand. If you have half yards, fat quarters, or smaller pieces, cut strips from those first, because they are easy to handle. I find a comfortable length to be from 8″ to 15″ and a good width from 1″ to 3″, but this is just a suggestion for starters.

If you are cutting from yardage, cut a 6″-wide swath and divide it into two pieces, each 22″ long. For this, you can cut freehand, use a ruler, or even tear the fabric. You're going to cut new strips from the 6″ × 22″ piece, so whatever you do is fine. In fact, the width of a strip doesn't even have to be the same from one end to the other.

Don't worry about color or value; just cut a variety.

Variety of cut strips

FREEHAND CUTTING AND SEWING

cutting strips of similar widths

1. Start with 2 strips of fabric approximately the same length. Place one fabric strip on top of the other, both right sides up, with the top long edge of one fabric ⅛″–½″ away from the bottom long edge of the other fabric and the left edges aligned. This does not have to be precise; just judge by eye.

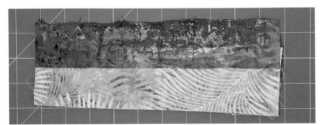

Place 2 strips, right sides up, one on top of the other.

2. Cut through both layers, close to the edge of the strip that is on top.

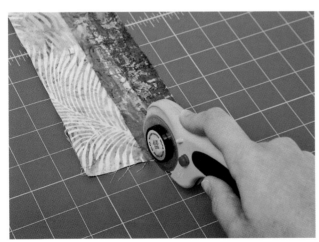

Cut through both layers.

3. Remove the excess fabric. Flip over the top strip so the right sides are together and the left edges are aligned.

Flip over top strip.

After you've flipped the top strip, you will see that the hills and valleys don't match on the long edge—that's the way you want them. They will be flat after they are sewn together.

Hills and valleys do not match.

cutting strips of different widths

1. Place the wider strip down first. Use the long edge *closest* to you as a guide and align the 2 bottom edges.

Place wider strip down first.

2. Cut close to the edge of the topmost layer and use the strip on the bottom left and the strip on the top right.

Cut close to edge.

3. As you did in Step 3 in Cutting Strips of Similar Widths (page 23), move the excess and flip the top layer so right sides are together.

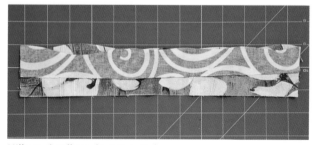

Hills and valleys do not match.

 Even though not all fabrics have a right and wrong side, you still need to flip one strip so the hills and valleys don't match as you sew; they will be flat after they are sewn.

sewing together free-cut strips

1. Make sure the ends where you begin to stitch are lined up. Don't worry about the rest.

2. Sew slowly, gently pulling the edge of the strip on top so the long edge aligns pretty well with the strip beneath. This will create a gentle curve in the seam. The edges don't have to be perfectly matched—just do the best you can. In the end, it won't matter.

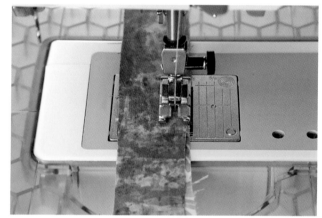

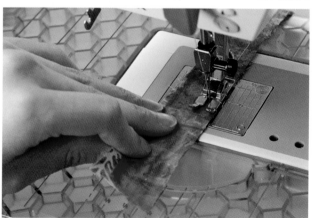

Maneuver strips so edges are together as you sew.

3. Open the seams and press. The seam will be gently curved, depending on how the edges were cut.

Open seams and press.

4. Repeat Steps 1–3 until you have 3, 4, or more strips sewn together. Not all strips will be the same length, because you either started with varying lengths or stretched one of the strips slightly as you sewed. This is normal. Don't trim them yet; we'll come back to them.

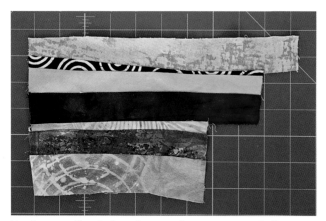

Don't worry if strip lengths vary, but try to sew similar lengths together.

don't worry about the ¼˝ seam

There is no rule that says you must use ¼˝ seams, and in many cases, you won't. In fact,

depending on the width of the strip(s), your seam may vary from one end to the other.

You might notice that the black-and-white strip in the photo (bottom left) is narrower than the others. It was ¾˝ wide and ended up about ½˝ wide finished. If you want a sliver of color, you can use a strip as small as ½˝ wide and make your seams ⅛˝.

starting with curved edges

Sometimes you'll have a random strip that has been cut in half, which results in both halves having a curved edge.

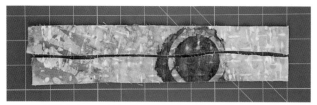

Strip cut with curved edges

1. Use the curve as a template for cutting another strip: Place one half (right side up, if there is a right side) on top of another piece of fabric and cut along the edge, following the existing curve.

Place cut strip on top of another strip and cut, following curve.

2. After you have cut the second strip, you'll have 2 curved halves of the second fabric. Take a strip from each set, place them right sides together, and sew.

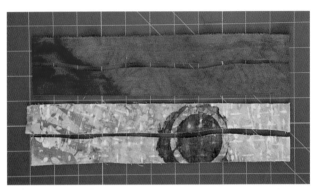

Matching curved-cut strips

3. Put the other mismatched set aside until later, when you might want to make them thinner or put something else between them for variety.

Keep cutting and sewing until you have strip sets in a variety of colors and sizes.

Strip sets

 You can cut two strips in half at the same time if, for example, they are 1½˝ wide and you want thinner strips.

Cut two strips at same time.

The resulting curved edges will be the same. If you decide to sew all four together, they will look like these stitched strips.

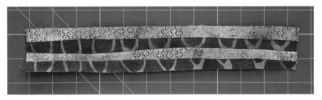

Stitched strips

No two sets will have the same curves. Often, there will be less of a curve in some of them or strips will not be the same width. Some will be narrower because they have been cut along both sides or are left over from another cutting. And sometimes a strip will be so narrow, it will barely be there. In fact, varying the widths creates interest.

Variety of strip widths creates interest.

 Make sure you sew together plenty of neutral strip sets in similar colors and values. These are great for giving your eye a place to rest between all the busy, colorful units you have made and are best made from solids, hand-dyes, or prints that read as solids.

Neutral strip sets

tip

The calming, read-as-solid strips on the left side of this lively piece by Linda Forey contrast perfectly with all the movement around them.

Untitled by Linda Forey, 19″ × 15″, 2010

TRIM THE ENDS

After you've sewn a bunch of therapy strips together, you have a launching platform for the next creative step. Remember those ragged edges I said not to trim?

Now it's time.

1. Trim the ragged edges from your strip sets and even them off.

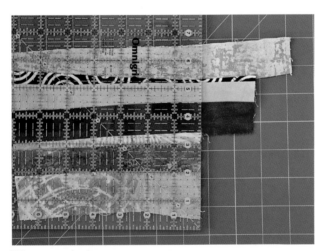

Trim ragged edges.

2. Measuring by eye, cut a slice (roughly perpendicular to your sewn strips) somewhere around 1½″–2″ wide.

Even up ragged edge and cut another strip.

In the next chapter, you'll see what you can do with your strip sets.

slice, dice, combine

There's no end to the ways in which you can transform a strip set into a variety of units. To give you a jump-start, I'm going to show you some of my favorites and some deceptively simple variations. No two units will be alike, and even slight differences in length, width, color, or value will give you an infinite assortment to play with. Once you get started slicing, dicing, and combining, it's like eating chips—you just can't stop. As long as you can cut strips freehand and sew them together, you're on your way! You can expect your path to meander as you take this journey, since there is no map. But I promise an adventure if you let yourself be guided by just two words....

"what if?"

"What if?" is the most important question you can ask yourself as you create original work. If you make those two words your mantra as you work, a world of possibilities will open up for you. You can't make a mistake, because you can always add, delete, or slice apart what you've made. And I predict you'll be so excited with the results that you won't be able to tear yourself away from your studio or sewing room.

variations on a theme

Begin with a simple set of strips you've sewn together. The following are only a few of the myriad variations you can make once you start to experiment.

TAKE A SLICE FROM A STRIP SET AND ...

Add a border to each side.

Then, *what if* you added a border to the top?

Or on all four sides?

What if you added a double border on the sides?

And single ones on top and bottom?

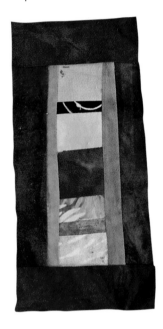

Or *what if* you added one only at the top?

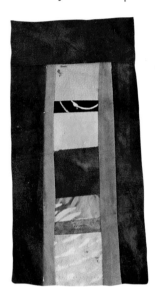

What if you changed the color of the top strip?

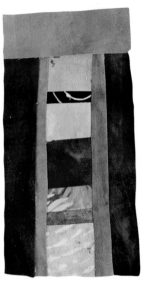

The emphasis shifts with the color change.

CHANGING PROPORTIONS

Varying size and shape can make a unit look entirely different. The construction process is the same, but look what happens when you make the units shorter, wider, or from a different palette.

Add double border on sides.

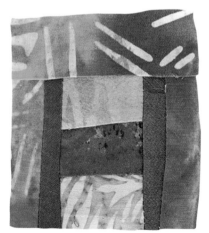

Add top strip.

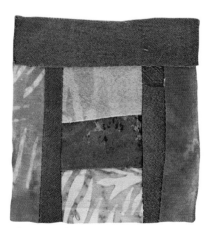

Change color of top strip.

What if your strips were all solids and the borders were a printed fabric?

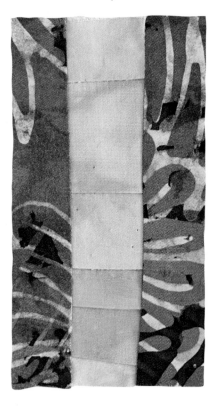

What if you alternated them and sewed them together to make stripes?

What if you sliced the stripes crosswise and randomly added several borders?

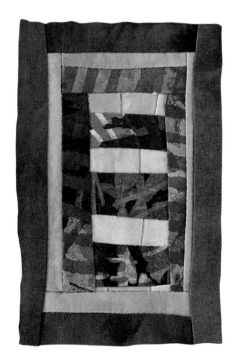

Look at a piece in different orientations. Doesn't each orientation feel different?

 It doesn't matter that the borders are different widths. Use what you have on hand—whatever you do is okay.

BUT, WAIT ... THERE'S MORE!

Instead of adding borders (or before doing so), cut the strip slice down the middle and add a solid.

The stripes won't always line up exactly once you have cut and resewn them, but that's not a problem. It just provides more interest. The same goes for uneven edges, which you don't want to trim yet.

What if you deliberately mismatched the strips by turning one side upside down before you attached it?

Or used two unrelated slices on either side of the solid strip?

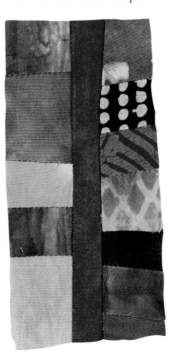

what's next?

Trying to show you where you can go from here is like giving you a recipe when I never cooked with one in the first place. But since this book is about working spontaneously (for the most part), it's part of the deal.

THE NO-RECIPE RECIPE

My grandmother never used a recipe for anything, and of course, nothing ever came out the same way twice. To get her butter cookie "recipe," I watched her and wrote things down as she did them. She used a glass (*6 ounces? 8 ounces?*) to measure the sugar and flour, then added "a pinch" of baking powder (*⅛ teaspoon? ¼ teaspoon?*) and a little more flour and sugar and baked "until slightly brown" (*temperature? time?*).

I guessed at the measurements and temperature, added vanilla and cinnamon, and kept mixing until it "felt" right and tasted good. My cookies weren't exactly like hers, but they were delicious. And, of course, my cookies are never the same twice either.

Here's my "no recipe" recipe for making some delicious, one-of-a-kind units that will also never be the same twice. That's the point!

1. Sew together a strip set of any length and width that feels comfortable. (Just for the record, I am working here with a set that is about 4½″ high and almost 4″ wide.)

2. Slice crosswise, anywhere.

3. Insert a strip or strips.

4. Rotate the unit a quarter turn and slice again.

5. Insert a strip across the first one.

6. If you reverse one end of the strip set before you sew in the second strip, it will look like this.

7. Either consider it done or repeat Steps 2 and 3 to cut again and insert another strip.

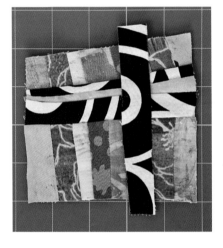

I opted not to insert another strip. Instead, I simply cut, reversed the left end, and sewed it back. Here is what it looks like now.

Although the result looks complex, it was really just a couple of cut-and-insert, turn-and-sew moves. Finally, I added a strip on each end and decided it was done.

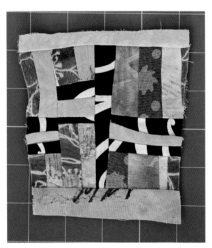

MAKING MULTIPLES

If your original strip set is anywhere between 12″ and 16″, you can cut it into three or four segments and do something different with each. This is an efficient way to work. You can use the segments separately and they'll relate, or you can sew two of them together and they will look even more complex.

Center varied by changing value and direction

Using multiples

Did I say the possibilities were endless? With just a few examples, you can see how changing one element can alter the original, sometimes dramatically. These variations can range from the simple to the complex, depending on how many times you cut them, what you add to them, what direction you turn them, and a host of other options. The piece that follows keeps it simple.

Just know ahead of time that every strip set and resulting unit will be unique; you will never be able to repeat any of them exactly because you are not measuring, using a pattern, or cutting with a ruler (except to trim at the end). However, you can make units that have a family resemblance if you take several slices from the same set of strips and use them in different ways. If you leave the larger part of the strip set intact, you will have another connection with the same fabrics.

I could write an entire book of "what ifs," but you will discover your own as you keep going and start to experiment.

a square is a square is a square

A square is a square is a square. But it becomes something else when you slice, dice, add strips, and start to play! What it becomes is up to you—the variations on this simple classic are limited only by your imagination.

Strips + squares = infinite variations

what size square?

If you have leftover squares from another project, start with those. It doesn't matter what sizes they are, because you are going to transform them into something new. You can start with 2″ squares, 5″ squares, or anything in between; how you change them will depend on your mood, your instincts, your fabrics, and your creativity.

If you don't have any spares, cut a 3″–6″ strip of fabric and slice it into whatever size squares or rectangles you want. You can use a ruler at this point, but after this, cut freehand until you are ready to trim.

what size strips?

Remember, there is no "should." If you are inserting a strip into a square or rectangle, anywhere from ½″ to 1″ wide is easiest to handle. Remember—you are measuring and cutting by eye, so widths are approximate and may vary slightly from one end of the strip to the other.

Inserted strip in square

Seam allowances can vary from ⅛″ to ¼″, depending on how narrow you want your insert.

If your seam allowances are approximately ¼″:

- A 1″-wide strip finishes around ½″.

- A ¾″-wide strip finishes around ¼″.

 A strip that starts around ½″ wide will be very skinny and may even disappear along the way. Sew with seam allowances of approximately ⅛″.

work quickly and intuitively

The secret to creating units that are exciting and unique is to work quickly and intuitively. Don't get bogged down in wondering how fat or skinny the insert strips should be or what colors you should use with what. Just do it! In the meantime, the following are some can't-miss ideas to start with. After you get going, you'll take off and run in your own direction.

SPLIT SQUARE

1. Place a random strip somewhere on the square, right side up. (The direction is important if there is a right and wrong side to the fabric. But if you forget and cut it face down, use it anyway—nobody will notice).

2. Cut the strip to the size of the square (or rectangle) and cut freehand through both fabrics. If the strip is very narrow, cut along the edge.

3. Set aside the narrow trimming and turn the insert strip face down along the edge of the square.

4. With right sides together, align the top edges and sew as you did with your strip sets (page 24).

5. Open, press, and sew the other part of the square to the strip.

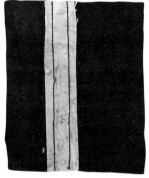

Remember, nothing has to be straight or exact—not the squares, not the strips, and not even the seams. Although you may want to use ¼″ as your general guide, it doesn't have to be perfect. You can even vary your seam allowance from one end to the other, which will vary the finished width of the strip—anything goes!

After you insert the strip, it will be slightly crooked, as you would expect when you cut without a ruler.

Strip before insertion

Strip after insertion

The insert does not have to be in the center of the square, and many times it won't be. You can put it anywhere you like!

Place inserts anywhere within square.

Nor does it have to be one piece of fabric. The insert (below) is a slice from a strip set.

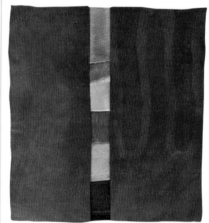

Strip set slice used as insert

THIN STRIPS

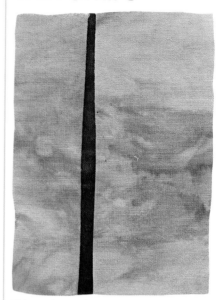

Thin strips make great accents.

When you work with thin strips, be sure to press the seam allowance toward the piece to which you sewed the thin strip. That way, it won't get caught when you sew the second seam.

Press seam toward larger piece.

When you sew the second seam, keep the insert side up so you can see how close you are to the other seam.

Keep insert side up when sewing.

It's better to press the seam allowances as you go along. Although I prefer to press the seam allowances in strip sets to one side, I always recommend pressing those of an insert, especially a very narrow one, away from the inserted strip. Notice here that the seams are not straight and are about ⅛″ wide.

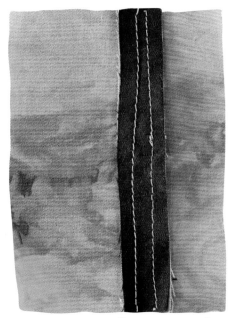

Press insert seam allowances away from inserted strip.

where to go from here

You can go almost anywhere as long as you're asking yourself, "What if?"

VARIATION 1
What if you added a crosswise strip?

Evenly centered inserts

Off-center inserts

VARIATION 2

What if you turned one half upside down before sewing it back together? Note that this works only if the square is divided unevenly, so the lines don't intersect when you turn one side in the opposite direction.

Turn one half of block around before sewing.

VARIATION 3

What if you added a second strip to the offset square?

Add second strip.

VARIATION 4

What if you reversed that right-hand segment top to bottom?

Reverse segment.

VARIATION 5

What if you started with two parallel inserts?

Add parallel inserts.

Okay, so they are not exactly parallel. Nor are they the same shape or width because you're cutting freehand; it just adds to the visual spontaneity. If you are inserting two strips, you'll need to cut them narrower than if you were inserting just one.

VARIATION 6

What if you added a strip or two in the other direction? (My husband called these shapes "those H's and tic-tac-toes on your wall.")

The "H"

The "tic-tac-toe"

VARIATION 7

What if you used diagonal inserts?

Diagonals add energy to all those squares and rectangles, so go ahead and insert one (or more). In Frauke Schramm's dynamic quilt, skinny strip set pieces and random diagonals create whimsy and a sense of energy.

Don't You Love a Good Mystery, Too? by Frauke Schramm, 27˝ × 37˝, 2009

When you work diagonally, your strip needs to be longer than the size of the rectangle or square so that you don't lose a lot of fabric when you trim.

A diagonal or two will liven up almost any block. You'll discover many other permutations when you play around with cutting, turning this way and that, and resewing.

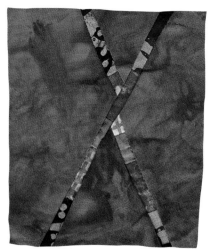

Diagonals liven up block.

WHAT IF YOU'D RATHER FUSE?

If fusing is your thing, be my guest! I don't do a lot of it, but I admit there are some things better done with fusing. If you have trimmings so narrow that you can't piece them, such as the ¼″ offcuts from an insert, just iron them to fusible web, drop them or place them on the square, and iron them down. My personal bias for this example would be toward pieced units. However, from a distance, the fused pieces work just fine after they are quilted.

Fused "insert"

what's next?

We've looked at inserting vertical and horizontal lines into a simple square (or rectangle), and we've turned the cut pieces so the lines don't intersect. But this is just the beginning, and I suspect your head is already full of other possibilities. Let's keep going.

add, subtract, multiply, divide

The framed square (or Square-in-a-Square) is not new or revolutionary. But it is another basic with great flexibility.

Like the neutral strips in Start Stripping (see the tip, page 27), simple framed squares are good places to rest the eye when a lot is going on around them. And they make excellent starting points for more interesting units. Of course, squares don't have to be perfectly square, because you're going to add to them anyway. And "squares" can just as easily be rectangles.

Framed squares

The improvisational sewing process of cutting, sewing, slicing, resewing, recutting, taking apart, and putting together pieces of fabric comes down to these four simple terms: *add*, *subtract*, *multiply*, and *divide*.

While these might sound mathematical, they are actually part of the creative process as you make original quilts. Think about it: You're *adding* one piece of fabric to another. If you decide you've added too much, you can take the excess away—*subtraction*. When you slice into the fabric to insert something, you're *dividing*. As you keep making units, they will *multiply* until you have enough to work with. Simple! I hope you'll use all these terms as inspiration while you continue to experiment. They are really part of the process.

add

Let's take our basic split square, add a cross-wise strip (page 41), and put a frame around it.

Start by adding strips of any size as a frame (or border, if you prefer). If the strips are too wide, trim them and hold on to the trimmings. If the edges are uneven but you are going to add more to the unit, don't use your ruler yet.

Add strips as frame.

If you keep adding, it gets better. Notice that I did not add to all four sides each time; this keeps it less symmetrical and more interesting.

Add additional strips.

As another possibility, add double strips to both ends; then place a frame all the way around.

When you are adding, the sequence doesn't matter. If you do what strikes you at the moment, each outcome will be unique.

Another framing possibility

And another framing possibility

Add frames to any bits in your box.

true confession 1

I had so much fun making these that I took a long play break before I came back to write about it.

true confession 2

I can't tell you how I made the center of this block because I don't remember. I just sliced, diced, turned, sewed, and repeated until I got something I liked. Then I added.

Slice, dice, turn, sew, add.

true confession 3

I *fused* the blue square to the center of the square. The two center squares were leftovers, and it made sense to use them. The yellow lines could have been fused, but I preferred to insert them. You, however, may make a different choice.

I took these framed squares a step further by combining them with some strip units and other fabrics. This could remain a 10″ × 10″ piece or become part of a larger work.

Fused blue square in center

Framed square + strip units and other fabrics

KEEP AN OPEN EYE
AND AN OPEN MIND

Look at the scraps and trimmings as you work, because they will often spark ideas. Just as you may have begun to look at found objects differently when you started to print with them, you'll see multiple possibilities as you slice and sew.

When I finished the following unit, I spotted the scraps I had trimmed from the borders and had an *aha!* moment: I could fuse one or both of the skinny strips to the center of the simple framed square.

Leftover trimmings

Trimmings fused as "X"

Trimmings fused as bars

If you have a spare square too small to cut or if you are feeling lazy, there's nothing that says you can't "fake" a framed square by fusing instead of piecing.

Square fused to square

subtract

Subtracting will come in handy when you are designing your quilt on the wall. During that important editing process, you'll find yourself moving or removing elements that aren't working. Or you might find yourself, seam ripper in hand, "unstitching" a strip or two or even cropping a finished piece.

multiply

Making multiples often happens by itself as you work with similar fabrics or while you experiment with "what ifs." Multiples are siblings, but they won't be identical, because you are cutting freehand. Even if you are using similar fabrics, they are not all the same. If there is a family resemblance, consider it a multiple!

ACCIDENTAL MULTIPLES

Sometimes, multiples result from a series of experiments that may not have worked the way you thought they would. But take heart—they will come in handy when you suddenly find that a few of them are just right for the latest project. And, of course, you can modify them later, when more inspiration hits.

true confession 4

The following were "what if?" experiments that didn't make it into the previous chapter. (They are pink—what was I thinking?)

However, since they use the same fabrics, they could lend a cohesive note to a piece or a series. And when I slice, dice, and change them, they will still have a common element, even if the added fabrics are not the same for each.

Here, I *divided* and then *added*. Much more lively, don't you think? Now it's the family clown.

Framed square that was divided and added to

Multiples

These orange and purple units count as multiples, even though they are not the same shape or size. You might call them "cousins."

Related multiples

By first combining these two and then slicing, dicing, and adding more fabric, you can create a more interesting unit than either is by itself.

Combine two units.

Slice, dice, and add.

You won't remember how you did it, but it doesn't matter. It's still one of the multiples and a lot more fun than the originals!

DELIBERATE MULTIPLES

Sometimes you will make a unit you like so much that you want to create another. In fact, as practice, it's a good idea to make two or three of almost any basic using similar fabrics or colors. None will be identical, because you are cutting freehand and improvising as you go. But there will be a family resemblance that will add unity to your work or enable you to do a series.

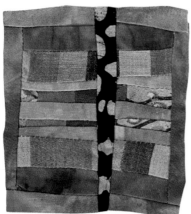

Deliberate multiples

Here are some other examples of working with the same palette, fabrics, or elements so you can use them in the same piece later on. The trick is not to think but just to slice and dice and reconfigure the blocks until they please you.

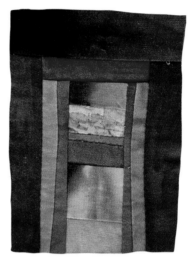

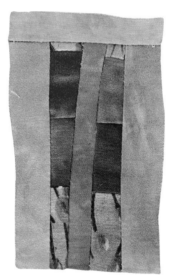

Deliberate multiples

Of course, yours will not look the same as these—they will reflect your hand, your personality, and your color sense—which is as it should be. These are merely examples.

divide

Most of your work will be adding and dividing— sometimes in the reverse order. You may find as you go along that an existing unit will work better if you divide it. In that case, get out the rotary cutter and go for it.

I divided the following after adding the frame, so the strip would go all the way through.

Divided framed block

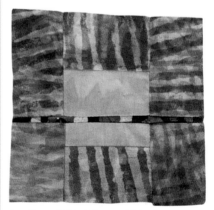

Another divided framed block

For these, I divided them first and then added their frames.

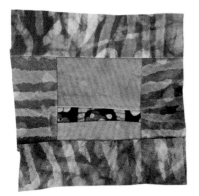

Divided, then framed

In this one, I added the dark strips, divided the square, and added to the top and bottom.

Dark strips added, square divided, top and bottom added

true confession 5

Here is another experiment from the cutting-room floor. I had made two units and didn't like them, so I divided one and rearranged the segments. Although I didn't like them any better, I kept them and later found a solution.

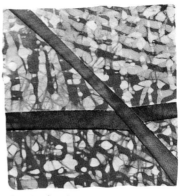

Original unit

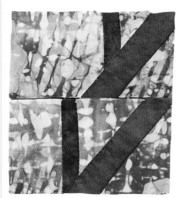

Divided unit variation 1

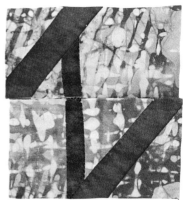

Divided unit variation 2

I added all three units together. Your solution would probably have been different, just as mine might have been different on another day.

Divided unit variation 3

As you can see, there is no one right (or wrong) choice. Your decisions will work themselves out when you get to the design phase and see what else is in your collection of bits, strips, and fabrics. For now, just make what pleases you and don't worry about how you will use it later.

fearless color

anything goes

Whether for sewing, knitting, embroidery, or crochet, my grandmother always had a needle in her hand. She had no issues with color; she used up her leftover yarns, threads, and fabrics in the next project, storing the bits left and using them again. If she had orange, purple, olive, and fuchsia leftovers, she used them together without worrying whether they "went" or not. Of course they "went"! Why shouldn't they? Any colors can work together if you use Nanny's fearless approach.

In her hands, the classic red/green combination became hot pink/
acid green, while green and yellow became turquoise and bronze.
These were decidedly not common color palettes in the 1950s,
when she made them.

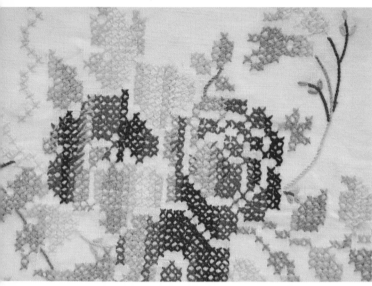

Classic red/green combination becomes
hot pink/acid green.

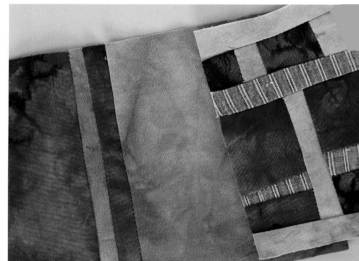

Common color combination green and yellow
becomes turquoise and bronze.

"Nanny," I said one day, "no matter what colors you put together, they always look beautiful. How do you do it?" Her answer: "Darling, there's no such thing as *doesn't go*. You can use any colors together as long as you repeat them somewhere." It was a lesson I never forgot.

The following quilt is a masterful example of Nanny's principle.

Most of us would not put maroon and gray next to turquoise and red. And we wouldn't think of putting orange and brown stripes next to red and pink stripes. But the colors go together because they are all repeated somewhere else and because there is a preponderance of red throughout, which draws the eye around and unifies the piece.

Nasturtium by Helene Davis, 33″ × 28″, 2007

you don't need a color wheel

I was in my 40s before I ever heard of a color wheel. When I asked what it was, somebody said it was so you'd know what colors went together. Out of curiosity, I bought one. It was very pretty and kept me amused for about fifteen minutes, but it didn't give me any new information other than the terms *analogous, complementary,* and *split complementary,* which had no meaning to me. I wondered why anyone would care what a color combination was called as long as it looked good.

how can you tell what works?

How can you tell what colors "work" together? Use your eyes! Children's drawings are perfect examples of fearless color. Kids can draw a person with *turquoise* hair, *orange* eyes, and a *blue* mouth standing next to a tree with a *green* trunk and *purple* leaves and not give it a second thought until some teacher "corrects" their view of color.

Child's view of color

The color scheme may not be realistic, but it works. If you have ever used a color wheel, you'll know that blue, green, and turquoise are analogous colors; orange/blue and green/purple are complementary colors; and orange, green, and purple are secondary colors. Children have instinctive and imaginative color senses. So do you, though you may have been taught to mistrust it.

trust your instincts

I was once in line behind a woman choosing fabric for a quilt. She had picked a pink, blue, and beige floral print, and her companion fabrics were solids in exact matches for those three colors. Did they go together? Yes. Were they deadly boring? To me, yes.

She timidly asked the shop owner's opinion, and the answer was "lovely." Unsolicited, I offered my not-so-humble opinion and suggested a bit of orange and acid green. The owner looked daggers at me and rang up the sale before the customer changed her mind. I suspect there was not a bit of orange or acid green in the shop.

leaving the safe zone

You could say the colors in this block go together; at least, they are safe choices. But when my friend Rachel unearthed them recently, she wondered what she had been thinking when she used this color scheme. "Hmmm," she said, "now I know why I stopped after making four."

Boring, abandoned block

I challenged her to do something with them. Determined to help her get rid of that cotton-candy sweetness, I grabbed a block and joined the challenge.

Since my objective was to minimize the pink, I sliced thin pieces and combined them with strips and units of other fabrics in my inventory. Was I thinking about which colors to add? Not consciously. But after I had finished the piece and analyzed the color choices, I realized there were warm (yellow-based) colors to counteract the cool pink and purple. In addition, I had added some darks to provide contrast.

By the way, the updated piece is a good example of having made units and strip sets without knowing how they would be used

later. The purple and orange tic-tac-toe unit (page 43) was perfect for this project, as was the strip set on the right.

My update of boring, abandoned block

Rachel and I worked separately and never saw the other's piece until we were done. Not surprisingly, she had also added strips of gold, acid green, and some darker values. But she went a step further and added red, which makes her piece sing.

Rachel's update of boring, abandoned block

making color choices

When you start sewing strips from scratch, you have unlimited choices. If you want to narrow down those choices, start with one color and cut strips in a variety of colors and values. These can be all solids or solids mixed with prints in the same palette. Sew three or four together to see how you feel about them. You may want to add, delete, or substitute a different color or two.

For *Waverunner 2,* Victoria Findlay Wolfe auditioned colors by hanging them together on her design wall. She substituted dark purple for the original black and dark brown and then added three turquoise zingers—unexpected touches. She did not need a color wheel for this vibrant quilt; she trusted her eyes.

Waverunner 2 by Victoria Findlay Wolfe, 48½″ × 45½″, 2009

BE FEARLESS WITH COLOR!

Pull out a pile of fabrics, cut strips, and try a wide variety to see what makes you smile. If you are working with prints, it is easy to pick up one or two of the colors. They look perfectly fine.

Print with "matching" solid

Step out of that comfort zone and try some unlikely or unexpected combinations. Don't be afraid to put varied colors and values together; just repeat one or more of the fabrics or colors somewhere else in the piece.

I started with two strips in my scrap box and tried several combinations.

But look how the print pops when we pair it with something unrelated or unexpected.

Print with unexpected solid

The first version was the easiest and safest—all those autumn colors went together very well. The results were attractive but predictable.

Print with unexpected print

Pretty, but predictable

How can you avoid this pitfall of predictability when selecting colors for your work?

It takes time, experimentation, and, of course, some judgment. But it's also fun to try fabrics and colors that you wouldn't reach for automatically.

If you really don't want to choose colors, try the paper bag trick, which you may have used for early scrap quilts and Log Cabins: Put darks and medium darks in one bag and lights and medium lights in the other. Then pick from the bags without looking.

It's a guilt-free process, because whatever you put together will ultimately work with something else. When you're done, toss the unit into your scrap box. Here's how my guilt-free paper bag piece turned out (really!) You can't go too far wrong with this method.

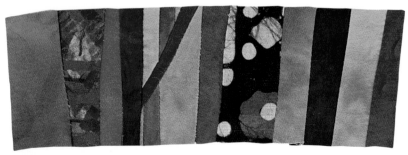

Blue strips bring in another color, and turquoise accents add jolts of brightness.

Black and white can perk up almost anything. When you're stuck, try it.

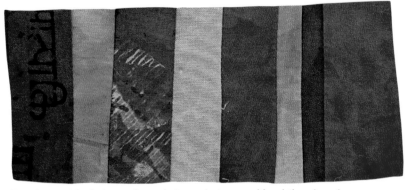

Purples and fuchsia are less obvious choices and lead the piece in another direction.

Guilt-free paper bag piece

color communicates

Color is the strongest visual element and is the first thing we notice. Whether or not we are aware of it, color establishes a mood.

The gray and blue in *Glacier Study #1* convey icy cold, which is exactly right for what Nancy Dobson is communicating. Imagine the same composition in hot pink and yellow; it would hardly make us think of a glacier.

Glacier Study #1: Crevasse by Nancy Dobson, 31½″ × 53½″, 2010

By the same token, the predominant yellow, orange, and bright pink in *Sunny Delight* provide an overwhelming sense of light and warmth, despite the gray in the other fabrics.

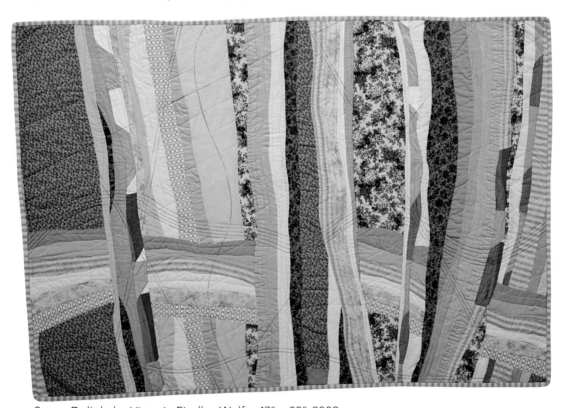

Sunny Delight by Victoria Findlay Wolfe, 47″ × 32″, 2009

Although these three pieces use the same floral fabric, the different colorways evoke different moods and responses.

Different colorways project different moods.

a word about value

As you know, *value* refers to the degree of darkness or lightness of a color. Although color is the most visible element, value is just as important. If all the values are too similar, the piece can be dull or difficult to read. Even low-contrast pieces can benefit from some shift in value.

Strata by Rayna Gillman, 42″ × 29″, 2009

Just as you used the black-and-white camera setting when sorting fabrics, you should use it as you design. This technique will tell you whether the values are what you want in a piece.

Because I wanted to communicate serenity, the colors and values are similar in most of this piece. Even so, it benefited from some darker and more vivid additions.

But it is not only the fabrics that have personalities; so do the pieces you make with them. As you work, you will see that the same bits and strips, even in similar colors, project different personas in solids or hand-dyes than in prints. A little unit in solids projects a sleeker and more contemporary look than the one made with prints, despite similar color and value.

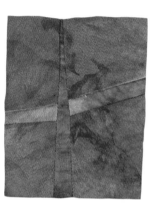

Print versus solid

For example, although the following piece contains some prints, it feels more contemporary than its companion piece (page 9, bottom right) because the majority of the fabrics are hand-dyed and read as solid.

Black-and-white photo of *Strata* shows value.

a word about personality

In addition to color and value, there's one more thing to mention: fabric personality. We all know that fabrics have personalities—lively, restful, noisy, quiet, outgoing, subdued, funny, serious, funky, old-fashioned, contemporary, and so on. I'm sure you can come up with your own adjectives. Part of that personality is color; another part is the type of pattern, floral versus geometric and so forth, which we won't go into here. Yet another element is solid versus pattern.

Hand-dyed fabrics project contemporary feel.

Don't obsess over fabric personality. It's just one more thing to observe and factor into the mix as you look at color and value.

creating a color bridge

When you are sewing strips, it's a good idea to make some sets that you can use as transitions from one palette to another. The following strip sets are all in the same general palette of peach / orange but with enough variety to work well with other color combinations.

This set works with a range of reds and purples because the warm brown with touches of red (in the center) provides a bridge to the orange-red.

This set works with golds and blacks because the same warm brown is a bridge to the golds.

Transition strip set

And turned around, the same strip set segues into soft blues that also have touches of peach.

Storm Warning by Rayna Gillman, 37″ × 18½, 2010

As you can see in *Storm Warning,* it's not about matching but about working together.

Designed ad hoc on the wall, *Storm Warning* uses color bridges to tie the elements together. It went up quickly, but then the process slowed down. This project rested on my wall until it was finished. In the last chapter of the book, you'll see how you can put ad hoc design and its partner—slow design—to work for you.

reinventing UFOs with strips and bits

The only thing more fun than creating original new work with strips and bits is using them to create exciting new work from UFOs (UnFinished Objects), or those blocks and tops languishing in a drawer or closet somewhere.

UFOs

We all have them—quilt tops that we were going to finish, along with a pile of random blocks, experiments, vintage flea market finds, baby quilt leftovers, and mismatched sizes in now-unappealing colors and fabrics. In fact, in Getting Started, I urged you to make a pile of these orphans and put them aside so you could come back to them. Now it's time.

Are you up to the challenge? All it takes is some minor surgery and then you have carte blanche. Reinventing is challenging and fun and will bring all your creativity into play, with *play* being the operative word. As you create new art from old blocks and tops, you are in charge, and nobody will tell you what you can or can't, must, should, or shouldn't do. Have some fun and experiment with your UFOs.

reinventing a block

Pieced blocks to reinvent

Pieced blocks are perfect candidates for reinvention. In essence, treat them the same way you treated the squares in the previous chapters: slice, dice, insert, reslice, rearrange, add, and see what develops. The good news is that because you are starting with a pieced block, it becomes more complex with the first cut and insert. Be fearless with your rotary cutter; you can't go wrong. The bad news? There isn't any!

I found eight or ten of the following scrappy vintage blocks in my steamer trunk. Since I failed to see their charm, I got out the rotary cutter. Nothing could make this block worse, so the idea was to *improve* it. With this in mind, I auditioned an endless variety of strips.

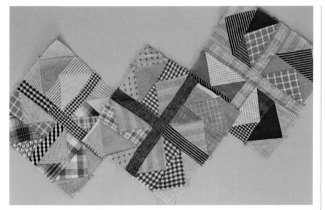

Original blocks

Here are two of the better choices.

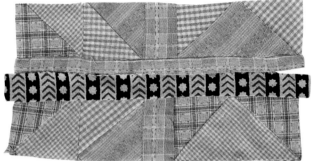

Option 1

Original block sliced

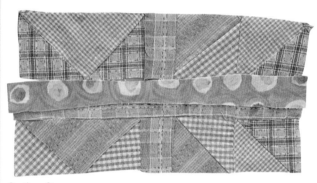

Option 2

After I had sliced, inserted, and rearranged a few times, I had several new units in different shapes and sizes.

 There's no rule that says you have to put the block back into one piece. In fact, you get more mileage out of the original if you have several related units to use.

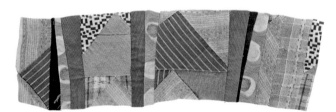

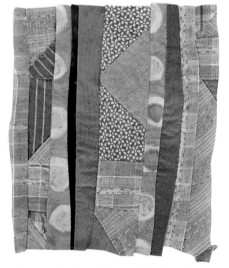

Cut-up blocks with new fabric added

USE WHAT'S AT HAND

Don't overlook the idea of taking apart other, unrelated blocks to recombine with the ones you are reinventing.

Here, I divided a leftover strip of triangles and used one section along with more recent fabric strips to reinvent the vintage block. Much better!

Leftover triangle strip

Triangle strip incorporated with vintage block

WHAT WAS I THINKING?

At some point, we've all asked ourselves, "What was I thinking?" When I look at this drab block, I can't imagine why I bought these fabrics or what I had in mind when I used them together.

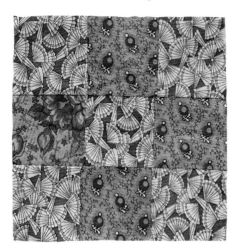

What was I thinking?

Individually, these reproduction fabrics were pretty bland, and combining them in a Nine-Patch didn't help. In the end, I used some of the fabric as background for an early art quilt. But what to do with the remainders? Slice, add strips, rearrange, and repeat. Remember, mistakes are impossible with this process: If you don't like it, you can always add or divide.

You also don't have to use the entire block when you rescue it. One of the segments from the strip in the middle became the center of a framed square; the rest of the section center will go into the box to be recycled and used later.

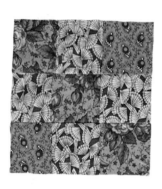

Is it worth the time to cut and paste these ugly blocks? Think of it as therapy sewing: You're improving the original, you don't have to do much thinking, and you are adding inventory to use creatively later.

Here are some reinventions of blocks created by slicing, adding strips, rearranging the pieces, and repeating the process.

This block cried out to be made into stripes.

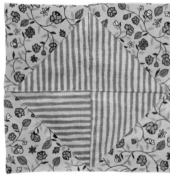

This block wanted to be funky.

A similar block went into the "witness protection program."

It may be hard to see the possibilities, but once you combine these reconfigured blocks with the strips, scraps, and other blocks in your box of leftovers, you'll see all kinds of potential. Just imagine the "witness protection" block topped with half of a leftover Log Cabin!

Reconfigured block topped with part of leftover Log Cabin

Cabana practically made itself with leftover blocks and strips. What fun!

Cabana by Rayna Gillman, 24″ × 30″, 2009
Photo by Rayna Gillman

reinventing a quilt top

A UFO, by its very nature, is still a work in progress, even if you have put it aside for twenty years or more.

WHY IS IT UNFINISHED?

- You didn't like it well enough to finish it.

- You ran out of one fabric and never found it again, so you gave up.

- You got halfway through piecing it and were bored.

- You never got around to quilting it, and now the fabrics look dated.

- It was a wedding gift, but before you finished it, they got divorced.

- A relative left it to you in her will. You hate it but feel guilty throwing it out.

- You've moved on to making original work and are stuck with these traditional tops.

I suspect you could come up with a few reasons I haven't thought of. But in the end, it doesn't make any difference *why* you have them. Now you can make them into original work.

A UFO is fertile ground for creativity. A top (even a partially finished one) offers several options for how you can take it apart and even more options for how you can put it back together into something new.

I don't know about you, but I have a couple of quilt tops I thought were the "cat's meow" when I made them. One is an early 1980s brown and pink Log Cabin I made for my daughter. Then she changed her color scheme and didn't want it. I haven't tackled that one yet.

Pink and Brown Log Cabin by Rayna Gillman, 1980

Another UFO was an Ohio Star with 15″ blocks and red calico sashing, which I have already taken apart. The blue fabric is 65% polyester / 35% cotton and has a sheen. Wait until you see what happened with this one!

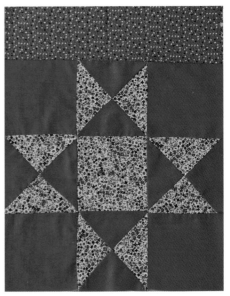

Old Ohio Star block

The third is a "What was I thinking?" top that I have since cut into, despite thinking it was too ugly to bother with. It's the same vintage as the Ohio Star—can you tell?

Old Log Cabin—a "What was I thinking?" quilt top

DECONSTRUCTING A UFO

Don't let a large quilt overwhelm you. Just take your rotary cutter and go! Yes, it's a bit daunting to cut into a completed top, but after the first slice, it gets easier. Here are some options for tackling the job.

slice along the seamlines

This method works well when you are not in the mood to sit down with a seam ripper and carefully separate every block from its neighbor. Go ahead and slice them on each side of the seamline; it won't matter a bit.

Slice next to seamline.

I gave a block to my friend Rachel, wondering whether she could save it.

Original Log Cabin block

Black, white, and beige to the rescue! She added so much that it's much larger than the original block and would make a great center for a larger quilt.

Transformed Log Cabin block

ignore the seamlines

Slice through the whole length or width of the quilt top without regard to how it is pieced, as if it were a wholecloth top. This works well when the piecing is irregular or when you just dislike the top so much you don't care how you cut it.

I had made six blocks using hand-printed cloth combined with a commercial fabric, but I hated the result. A well-meaning friend advised me to cut my losses and throw it in the trash.

Original blocks
Photo by Rayna Gillman

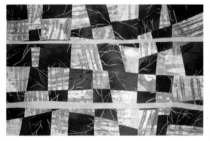

Two strips inserted
Photo by Rayna Gillman

After multiple additions and rearrangements
Photo by Rayna Gillman

Instead, I sliced all the way through the completed top, inserted strips, and was on my way, knowing that if it didn't improve, I could toss it later. Here are some stages in my "strips to the rescue" process.

Two strips added in other direction
Photo by Rayna Gillman

Finally, I fused some branches to the top and added a border. Done! I had made a silk purse out of a sow's ear.

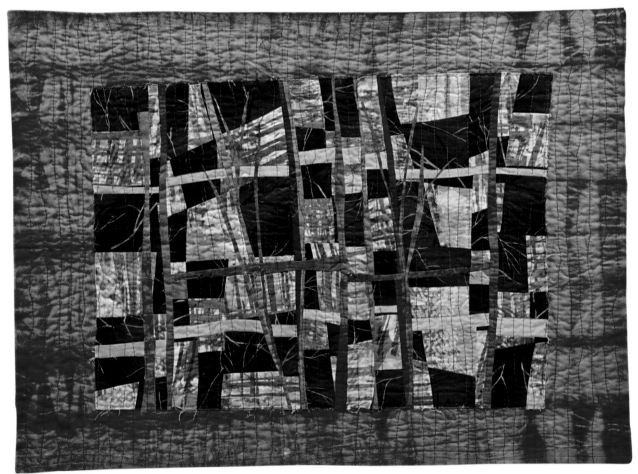

Sow's Ear by Rayna Gillman, 30″ × 21″, 2008
Photo by Rayna Gillman

sometimes, strips are not enough

Original quilt top
Photo by Rayna Gillman

Green strips added
Photo by Rayna Gillman

When I sliced this "dog" through each row and inserted green strips, it didn't help.

Adding more, but not liking it better
Photo by Rayna Gillman

So I cut again, inserted more, and turned the quilt slices every which way before I sewed them together again. Not much better.

Now we're getting somewhere.
Photo by Rayna Gillman

I realized I would never like this unless I chopped it up and combined it with other things, so I dug into my box of leftover therapy strips and units and started to play on my design wall.

Detail
Photo by Rayna Gillman

I was onto something. This is the value of having a box full of strip sets and squares enhanced with additions and alterations. Pull them out, combine them with some UFO slices, and put the magic of therapy sewing to work!

The process was a joy, as was the unexpected result. The original is hardly recognizable in the new piece. It is one I would never have made from scratch, and yet it became the first in an evolving series.

Urban Storefront by Rayna Gillman, 34″ × 29″, 2010

separate the blocks neatly

If you are not in a hurry or need some hand work to do while watching TV or sitting in doctors' offices, use your seam ripper to deconstruct the quilt top. This antique quilt got a sparkling makeover when the rows were reattached to bright red strips.

Birthday Wishes Redo by Victoria Findlay Wolfe, 65″ × 56½″, 2008

reconstructing a UFO

When I took apart my 1970s Ohio Star quilt, I removed the sashing with a seam ripper and separated every block, carefully keeping the triangle points intact so I could use some of them again.

If you have a box of bits and pieces, dig into them and see what you find. You may recognize the extra orange and purple multiples from earlier (page 49). I didn't know when or how I could use them, but they were just right for these reinventions.

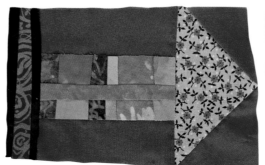

Reinvented Ohio Stars

Original Ohio Star block

CREATING LEFTOVERS AS YOU GO

Sometimes you won't have exactly the right colors or shapes to use with a block or top you are reconstructing. In that case, you can take a break and create some new units or strips that will fit the bill. As I was working with a section of the Ohio Star, I made an extra strip set (lower right in the adjacent photo). The other strips came from inventory. Working spontaneously also means stopping and making what you need at the moment!

Another Ohio Star reinvention

MAKE LEMONADE FROM LEMONS

On a whim, I invited blog readers to join me in the Ohio Star block challenge. As part of the challenge, I sent out the rest of the blocks to volunteers who wanted to play and create something new. There were no rules, and they didn't have to use the entire block in their new piece. Here are just a few of the inventive results that ended up as new quilts!

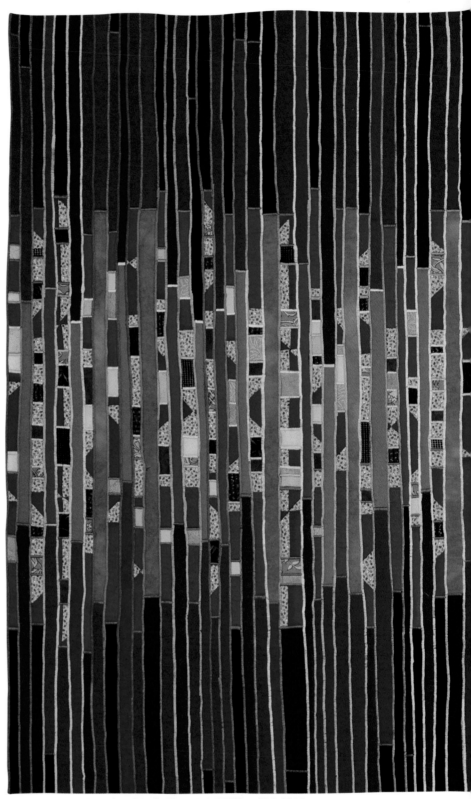

Once Upon a Time by Cécile Trentini, 23½″ × 39″, 2010
Photo by Fotohaus Peyer, E. Föhr

RG Redux by Karen Stiehl Osborn, 20˝ × 20˝, 2010

Old Star, New Tricks by Jennifer Beaven, 23˝ × 23˝, 2010

It is especially interesting that all three of these artists used strips to create their new work, because I never said a word to them about using strips to rescue these blocks.

A FEW THOUGHTS

Whether you're remaking a whole quilt or just a few blocks, here is some advice from veteran UFOer Rachel Cochran. When you are reinventing:

- Don't try to match or stay in the same color palette as the original. Add a color you think doesn't fit and then add it again.

- If you are used to planning before you cut, pull out a pile of fabrics, cut strips, and then see what fits, what you like, or what works.

- You need contrast, so vary your values (dark–light) and your temperatures (warm–cool).

- If you don't like it after you sew it, keep going. Cut again and insert something you will like. In the end, you won't even notice what you didn't like.

- Cut in another direction—for example, horizontally or diagonally if all your cuts are vertical.

- Don't second-guess yourself—you'll have a chance to decide what stays and what goes when you compose it on the wall.

Remember, this is play! Have fun with it, try not to overthink, and don't take it too seriously. This is a great way to be creative while waiting for inspiration from your usual muse.

Photo by Rayna Gillman

designing on the wall

If you are used to knowing ahead of time the subject of the piece, the size, or how you want it to look, this spontaneous way of working will be a change for you. Even if you prefer planning everything ahead of time, try working without plans and see what happens. Begin by sewing "therapy" strips and you may be pleasantly surprised as you go through the discovery process.

the vertical advantage

The floor works fine if you are laying out a traditional quilt, because the blocks are usually the same size. If they are identical, placement doesn't matter; if the colors or patterns are different, you can move them around easily until the arrangement pleases you.

It is a different story, however, when you are working spontaneously with units, strip sets, modules, and pieces of cloth, because they are almost always different sizes and shapes.

Designing on the wall will allow you to:

- Move pieces around instantly without having to bend (a real plus!).

- Photograph the variations easily and frequently.

- Step back from the work to see it from a distance as you go along.

If your room isn't big enough to give you good distance, use a reducing glass or your digital camera to see the work better. In fact, it's a good idea to do both, if you can.

meet your design partners: ad hoc and slow

Ad hoc design and slow design work hand in hand, whether you are starting from scratch with bits and strips, using a piece of fabric for inspiration, or creating new art from old blocks and tops. While you are working on the wall,

you will find yourself alternating between the two, which is as it should be.

AD HOC DESIGN

In this context, *ad hoc* means "improvised." No sketches ahead of time, no computer printout, and no concrete plan of how it will turn out—just working as needed or as the spirit moves you; designing as you go.

Throughout the book, I've encouraged you to work spontaneously (the "just do it" factor)—cut without a ruler, pick random strips, and start sewing; slice and dice without planning; trust your instincts with colors; don't overthink; and so on. That is all the ad hoc part of the process. You started working ad hoc when you sewed strips together without any planning. You worked ad hoc when you sliced up that UFO without a grand plan and when you spontaneously created, added, divided, and multiplied.

You didn't worry about how you were going to use those units or strips, knowing that at one point they would become part of new work. And now you are going to make *modules* from some of them and put them on the wall without knowing what the end result will be. This is ad hoc design.

creating modules

Modules are flexible building blocks that can be put together in any number of ways, depending on your aesthetic and how you'd like to use them. Call them segments, sections, components, or building blocks, if you wish. Whatever term you prefer, they are what results when you sew several smaller or different-sized units together to make larger ones. Using any unit as a starting point, you can work ad hoc, trying a variety of combinations spontaneously and using "what if?" as your guide. Some will work for you, some won't. Either way, this trial-and-error process may also give you some other ideas for later.

This photograph shows part of something I had cut into three pieces, thinking I could create three modules that related to each other.

Audition 1

Audition 2

Original

Audition 3

The first three auditions were fine, but the fourth and fifth auditions were better.

Audition 4—better

Audition 5—better

try this

Take a few units you've made and create two or three modules by combining them with strips or other units. Once you have several you like, put them on your design wall, along with other pieces you think might work with them.

Put modules and strips on wall.

Put them together ad hoc. Then add, subtract, and move the pieces around as you play with design and placement. Remember to take pictures as you go.

If nothing strikes you at the moment, take the pieces down but upload the pictures to your computer. Sometime later, take a look at the images; you may see the modules differently and realize that one of them was better than you thought and that you need to go back to it to continue working.

Play with your pieces.

Remember to take photos as you play.

SLOW DESIGN

Rarely does a piece make itself, though it may sometimes seem that way. When the composition appears to come together 1-2-3, it is probably because you have let it percolate on the wall and, often without realizing it, in your head. This is the best part of the slow design process—you don't even know you're working, and all of a sudden you know how the piece should come together.

Let's look at how *JazzFest* looked when I started working on it. In my ad hoc mode, I had put everything but the kitchen sink on the wall. Some of it stayed, but I had to sit back, listen to it, and let slow design do its thing.

JazzFest design process
Photo by Rayna Gillman

JazzFest design process
Photo by Rayna Gillman

Along the way, there was a lot of paring down, editing, and repositioning. But it paid off. The rhythm and shape of the finished piece make it evident that slow design had taken over as I worked.

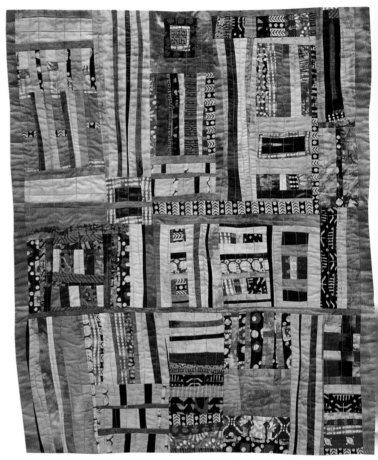

JazzFest by Rayna Gillman, 31˝ × 36˝, 2009

While *JazzFest* may look complex, it was not difficult to construct. Some of the units became modules before I put them on the wall. For the rest, I stopped as I went along and sewed them together into larger sections. Once I had assembled the sections, the rest was easy.

Look more closely and you will see a series of modules made from smaller units and strips. By now, you will probably find it easy to figure out how they were created.

JazzFest detail 1

JazzFest detail 2

good composition needs slow design

The best compositions are rarely easy to create. Often, the simpler the piece, the longer it has taken to arrive at. *Parameters*, with its clean lines and carefully combined strips, bits, and modules, belies the time and complexity behind the quilt.

Slow is the yin to ad hoc's yang—the two processes complement each other, and you will use them both. While you worked quickly and intuitively at the beginning as you cut, sewed, and cut again, you will want to slow down at a point and take all the time you need to reflect.

Parameters by Helene Davis, 25″ × 32″, 2007

reflect on the work

Reflecting is an important part of the process.

- Contemplate what is on the wall and ask yourself what else it needs.

- Add pieces, take others away, move them around.

- Think about composition, color, and value.

- Photograph anything that is a possibility.

- Walk away for a time and come back for a fresh look.

engage with it

Engaging with the work is critical, so don't rush it. If you are impatient to finish the piece and don't take the time to let it percolate, you may not do your best work.

- Listen to the work as it "talks" to you. A successful piece is a collaboration between you and the cloth, so let it sit on the wall for as long as it needs to.

- Have a visual dialogue with your work. Does it need to be bigger? Smaller?

- Engage with it. Is it better as a horizontal? A vertical?

let it evolve

As you contemplate and watch the piece evolve, take pictures at every step. You may think you will remember what it looked like at various stages, but you won't.

- Audition other fabrics or modules together.

- Rearrange things.

- Move pieces around to balance color, value, and composition.

- Sew together more strips if you need to fill in some spaces.

- Look at it from another direction (which is easy to do if you have taken photos).

- Take more time to contemplate.

- Take everything down and start fresh if you need to.

evolution of a piece: ad hoc to slow

Here are the beginnings of *Strata*, which I had "thrown" at the wall ad hoc.

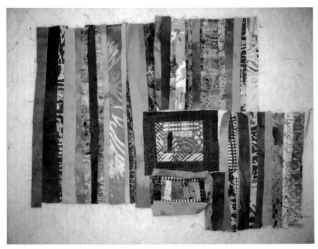

First attempt
Photo by Rayna Gillman

These multiples were fun, but not all together.
Photo by Rayna Gillman

Less busy combination
Photo by Rayna Gillman

By the time the strips ended up in the finished piece, everything had changed. What began as a vertical piece had become horizontal. Strip sets were sliced and distributed around the piece to support each other.

Photo by Rayna Gillman

Pieces were added, subtracted, divided, and repositioned. Modules were sewn together—three or four units at a time—and put back on the wall.

The work took on a less chaotic look as I sewed together strip sets and added them to fill out the piece and tie it together. Once again, modules were subtracted, added, and moved again. Blank spots appeared and had to be filled.

Photo by Rayna Gillman

Photo by Rayna Gillman

Strata by Rayna Gillman, 42″ × 29″, 2009

Sewing adjoining pieces into modules as you go makes the construction easier to manage.

TAKE PICTURES AS YOU GO

I can't emphasize this enough! Your digital camera is your best friend through this process because you can use it to record anything that is even a remote possibility. Keep it by your side; otherwise, later you will never remember what you had on the wall with what and in what sequence, proportion, or position. If you want to go back to one of the fabrics or one of the compositions you tried, you will need a photo to jog your memory.

working with hand-printed cloth

If you have hand-prints and hand-dyes, you have probably incorporated them into your bits and strips and units. But what if you want to use your hand-prints as starting points?

FIND A FABRIC THAT INSPIRES YOU

Often, the impetus for a quilt will be a piece of cloth that you love or find interesting, whether you've printed it or purchased it. *Green* started with a windmill hand-print made by Beverly Hart. It is a simple, effective showcase for the fabric, as well as an implied environmental message.

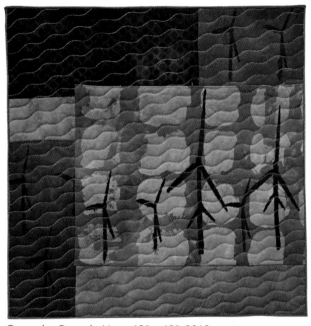

Green by Beverly Hart, 12″ × 12″, 2010

Snow-dyed cottons were the impetus for this quilt, and Norma Schlager made "wiggly" strips to complement them. Then she added the silks and dye-grabbers.

The starting point for *Fractured Forest* was a photo printed on cloth. Nancy Dobson searched through her hand-dyes for the colors she wanted to use, without having an advance idea of placement. Working without a sketch, she let the fabric tell her what to do—a perfect example of ad hoc design.

Spring Thaw by Norma Schlager, 27″ × 37″, 2010

Fractured Forest by Nancy Dobson, 10¼″ × 16¼″, 2008

Occasionally, you may want to challenge yourself with a fabric you dislike. Put it up and leave it there while you go through your other fabrics and modules. Sometimes, the fabric's color, motif, or mood will suggest a direction. Other times, you may need to work a bit to find out where you're going with it.

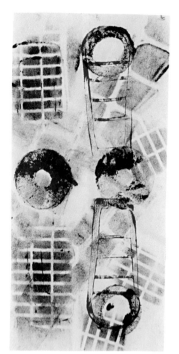

Original piece of fabric

Audition 1

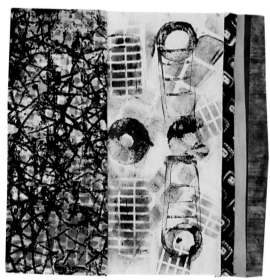

Audition 2

Despite auditions, the jury is still out on this one. The other half of the focus fabric ended up combined with other hand-printed fabrics, strips, and red-and-white units that you may recognize from page 42.

Rescue Squad by Rayna Gillman, 12″ × 12″, 2010

PIN IT UP

Put your inspiration fabric on your design wall. If you have limited space, start with a small piece, or fold and pin it before you put it up. I find that a half yard or less is easiest to start with, no matter how large the wall.

PULL OUT EVERY POSSIBILITY

Go through your stash and make a pile of fabrics you think might work with your starting point. You might end up with something completely unexpected.

START THROWING

I tell people to throw fabrics at the wall to see what sticks (although pins help). Do the fabrics play well together? Sometimes you will like more than one combination. In that case, it's a matter of trying other fabrics to see what else works with them. Keep an open mind, ask yourself "what if?", and try a lot of options—even fabrics you don't think will work. Pick a time when you are relaxed; if you're working with a deadline, the stress may prevent you from feeling free to play and experiment.

QUESTIONS TO ASK YOURSELF

As you audition companions for your fabric, here are some things to consider:

Original fabric

Do the fabrics play well together?

What if you added more fabric?

What if you changed their positions?

What if you added some strips?

What if you subtracted something?

What if you changed the orientation?

What if you changed the proportions?

When you have a series of audition photos, you might want to pick your two top favorites and see where each one leads you. This is where slow design plays its part.

You may find, to your surprise, that your second choice will be the start of a more successful and interesting piece.

putting it together

Once you start sewing the pieces together, you'll have some surprises in store and may find yourself working ad hoc again.

BE PREPARED FOR CHANGE

As you have seen, there is always an evolution from the ad hoc starting point through the slow design phase. Sometimes you may find that you have everything placed exactly right on the wall—it all looks great, it is the right size, and all the pieces look as though they fit. However, when you start to sew the pieces together, everything changes.

- Pieces that overlapped when you put them on the wall don't really fit, and you have to trim (or add to) them.

- When modules are sewn together, they suddenly get smaller.

- One fabric you wanted to show disappears in a seam.

- The more seams you have, the greater the shrinkage.

- As you put the pieces back on the wall, they suddenly seem too crowded.

- You need to stop and make (or find) some additional strip sets or modules because there is now a gap in the piece.

Therapy sewing to the rescue with more strips to fill the gaps! This is where you started, isn't it? Once again, you may have to slice, dice, reconfigure, audition, contemplate, evaluate, add, subtract, multiply, divide, and reorganize. Finally, some time later, you will end up with a piece that makes you happy.

Now you know that whenever the muse deserts you or you need time to unwind, you can jump-start your creativity by sewing strips and going on from there. Try taking a twenty-minute therapy sewing break at least three days (or evenings) a week, and pretty soon you'll have a box full of bits, strips, and "leftovers" waiting for you when you're ready to play. I promise, magic will happen! Trust the process.

about the author

Rayna Gillman works in mixed media on fiber, using a variety of surface design, collage, and printmaking techniques to integrate text and images into her work.

Photo by Irene Halsman

She made her first scrap quilt in 1974, when she fell in love with an antique quilt she could not afford. Over the years, she began to print her own fabrics and became intrigued by the textures and design potential of such items as corrugated cardboard, construction fence, and kitchen tools. Today, using found objects from the house, the hardware store, and even the street, she paints, dyes, and discharges, working in layers to add complexity to her highly recognizable fabrics.

Noted for her instinctive sense of color and her improvisational approach to design, she encourages students to work spontaneously, to experiment, and to use the question "what if?" to guide them. She has taught hundreds of students not only to print their own fabrics but also to use those fabrics creatively in their quilts.

Rayna was a featured artist on the TV show *Simply Quilts* and has written for *Quilting Arts Magazine*. In addition, her work has been widely published. She was a juror for the national Art Quilts Lowell show and teaches internationally. Her fabric and quilts have been exhibited in museums and galleries around the country and are in private collections in the United States, France, and Belgium.

She invites you to visit her blog and see her quilts at studio78notes.blogspot.com. You can reach her at rgillman@studio78.net.

resources

Andover Fabrics, Inc.
www.andoverfabrics.com

Aurifil USA
www.aurifil.com

Fairfield Processing
www.fairfieldworld.com

Handloom Batik
www.handloombatik.com

Helene Davis Hand-Dye Fabric
www.hand-dye.com

Michael Miller Fabrics, LLC
www.michaelmillerfabrics.com

OLFA—North America, a division of World Kitchen, LLC
www.olfa.com

Also by Rayna Gillman:

Great Titles *from* C&T PUBLISHING

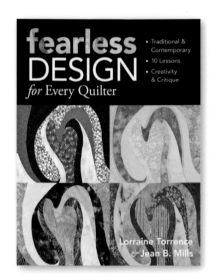

Available at your local retailer or **www.ctpub.com** *or* **800-284-1114**

For a list of other fine books from C&T Publishing, visit our website to view our catalog online.

C&T PUBLISHING, INC.

P.O. Box 1456
Lafayette, CA 94549
800-284-1114

Email: ctinfo@ctpub.com
Website: www.ctpub.com

C&T Publishing's professional photography services are now available to the public. Visit us at www.ctmediaservices.com.

Tips and Techniques can be found at www.ctpub.com > Consumer Resources > Quiltmaking Basics: Tips & Techniques for Quiltmaking & More

For quilting supplies:

COTTON PATCH

1025 Brown Ave.
Lafayette, CA 94549
Store: 925-284-1177
Mail order: 925-283-7883

Email: CottonPa@aol.com
Website: www.quiltusa.com

Note: Fabrics used in the quilts shown may not be currently available, as fabric manufacturers keep most fabrics in print for only a short time.